Ten Easy Days in Yellowstone:
A Geezer Guide

with Badger Bob
and the Professor

Ten Easy Day Hikes in Yellowstone: A Geezer Guide

ISBN number 1449519105. EAN-13 is 9781449519100.

Printed in the United States of America.

Cover and interior design: Thomas Graphics

Animal photographs: Nature's Eye Photography

Contacts: kenton.miller@yahoo.com

　　　　　　http://geezer-guide.blogspot.com

Dedication

This book is dedicated to our long-suffering wives, Tommye Kaye and Sharon Claire. Without their patience and understanding of our endless back-country adventures, this book could never have been written. Thanks guys, you're the greatest!

Acknowledgements

The authors gratefully acknowledge the contributions of the following people without whom this book would have been a poor thing indeed:

First and foremost we want to thank Ms Janie Thomas of Thomas Graphics who designed the cover and interior layout of this guide, and spent many hours revising text and placing photos.

We must also give a lot of credit to our good friend Ms Peggy Hamlen of Nature's Eye Photography who supplied all of the animal pictures in this guide (except where noted). In the authors' opinion, Peggy's animal photography is unsurpassed.

Expert editorial assistance was also provided by the authors' wives, Tommye Winters and Sharon Miller. No comma went unchecked, but if any errors remain, the blame rests entirely with the authors!

We also want to thank our long-time hiking buddy, Gene Ball, who critically reviewed an early draft of the guide and made useful suggestions on the title.

The authors thank Darry and Terry Shaw for designing the logos for Geezer Gear and Badger Bob.

Finally, the authors want to acknowledge the contributions of Ms Cathy Russell and Ms Cindy Mellott of the Yellowstone Association for reading the text and providing encouragement when it was sorely needed.

Preface

This is a different type of hiking guide. Most guides are written by professional outdoor people in great physical condition with considerable woodland craft and hiking skills. These men and/or women are very knowledgeable about hiking and camping and they usually assume their readers are in the same physical and mental condition as themselves. While this may be true for most of their *intended* readers, it's certainly not true for most everyday folks, and such guides sometimes have greater expectations about the physical abilities and trail skills than older or less experienced hikers can meet.

Not this guide! It is written for people who, like the authors, are either a bit "over the hill" or not in the best physical condition. This guide should be very useful for the first time hiker and folks who might like an easier or shorter hike. It's also great for families who may have "little ones" in tow.

The hikes in this guide can be done by almost anyone in reasonable physical condition. Most of the trails are not heavily used. The color photos and clear trail descriptions make it easy to achieve your goal. The humor may give you smile. There are also interesting stories and useful information about the Park. These hikes give the hiker a real feeling for the Yellowstone backcountry. That is the point and real purpose of this trail guide.

Each hike has been selected with several different things in mind. Most important was that ***none of these hikes are too difficult to do.*** If a Geezer can't make the hike, that hike won't be in this guide. No hike is longer than four miles. This may seem like quite a way, but it really is not. Most folks can cover this distance in a couple of hours of light walking. That leaves plenty of time for picture taking, flower smelling, talking, snacking, and resting.

The second consideration was beauty. Each of these hikes presents an awesome and seldom seen aspect of Yellowstone. The Park is a land of many gorgeous faces. The Geezer, first timer, or family who completes any of these hikes will experience some of Yellowstone's seldom seen faces 'up close and personal'.

The third consideration was variety. There is much to see and do in Yellowstone Park. Unfortunately, there is not enough time to see and do as much as you might like. This guide condenses opportunity and variety. Time is short and choices must be made. This guide makes the choices easy.

The final important consideration was safety. None of these hikes are long. The trails are clearly marked, so it's not difficult to find your way. The paths are relatively level and well maintained. There are no large obstacles to avoid. You don't have to "bushwhack" through rough terrain to reach your goal. The guide includes color photos, clear trail descriptions, and maps for good orientation and direction. However, most of these hikes are in the 'backcountry' where you will be on your own. You must use caution and good judgment for your own protection. The amazing things you'll see and do out-back make this guide worthwhile.

Over three million people visit Yellowstone Park each year, yet fewer than one percent of these visitors get farther than five hundred feet from a paved road or boardwalk. This is a great tragedy. They miss so much. Most people want to see and understand what Yellowstone is really about, yet most are hesitant to do so. Why? The answer is FEAR – Fear of the unknown, fear of getting lost, or fear of an animal confrontation. **These fears are unnecessary.**

You do **_NOT_** have to be afraid to see the real Yellowstone. You are in more danger driving your car on the highway than hiking in Yellowstone. Don't be afraid to visit the backcountry. The out-back will overwhelm your senses,

challenge your mind, and purify your heart. It will free you from the "hustle and bustle" of the highway and city. Once you've been out-back you'll want to go back again. You'll be welcome.

Happily, you don't have to venture very far to get "out-back". This guide will lead you to an authentic backcountry experience. Here are some questions to think about. Would you like to see the amazing Yellowstone backcountry? Are you ready for unique Park experiences? Does the idea of Yellowstone's majesty arouse your curiosity? If your answer is yes, to any of these questions, this guide is for you.

Table of Contents

Introduction

Almost everyone visiting Yellowstone Park has come to see the spectacular sights, especially those that are easily accessible from the Grand Loop Highway. Many visitors will see amazing thermal features, wild animals, wildflowers, waterfalls, mountains, lakes and more. The Grand Loop Highway was designed for easy access to these features.

But there is much more to see and do in Yellowstone. This is what this guide is about. The color photos and clear trail descriptions make the hikes easy to find and fun to follow. You may enjoy the stories and information about the park. There is even a chuckle or two to point out the fun in hiking the backcountry. The purpose of this guide is to encourage you to take the hikes and see the sights. You will soon find that backcountry hiking is not that difficult and the rewards are immense.

Of course, you will want to visit Old Faithful, the Grand Canyon of the Yellowstone, and Mammoth Hot Springs. All these marvelous attractions are definitely well worth your time. However, there are other wonderful and amazing places in the Park. These unique wonders lie off the beaten track in the backcountry. Most people who visit the Park will never encounter them. Whether it's time or timidity, these visitors will not leave the boardwalks to behold these wonders.

See the great attractions, but take some time to see the seldom seen Yellowstone. Over time, your warmest Yellowstone memories may be the ones to which this guide has led you. If you share your experience with others, this may encourage them to take a hike in the back country. They too will make memories.

The hikes in this book are not difficult, but that does not mean you should take them unprepared. Yellowstone is a land of many moods and, like a lady, she may change her mood without notice. Don't assume that a bright sunny day will continue to be bright and sunny until you arrive back at your car. The boy scouts were right. The first rule of hiking in Yellowstone is "be prepared."

Here are some suggestions for minimal hiking equipment. Take what you need with you. Don't leave safety to chance.

To start off on the right foot, you need a good pair of **walking shoes**. They don't have to be expensive, but they should be supportive with a solid sole that will grip the surface. Shoes should be "broken in", so they're comfortable and won't cause blisters.

Tennis shoes will work, but are not recommended. The soles are too thin (those stones can hurt!). Stylish "sneakers" don't supply enough support. "Low top hikers" are a good choice. They have thick soles with heavy toe guards. You know your own feet, so choose well.

The next consideration is **clothing**. A polyester long sleeve shirt and hiking pants are the best option. This type of clothing protects you from sun and biting insects. Polyester clothing also promotes efficient evaporative cooling. Being cool is important in summer weather. Some folks wear tee shirts, jeans, shorts and sneakers and they do all right on hikes. It's your choice.

Another important item is a **pack**. Your pack will carry most of your necessities. Either a shoulder pack or the more recently developed "fanny pack" will work. A shoulder pack can be easier to carry and hold more than a fanny pack. Shoulder packs with shoulder straps, hip belts and chest straps need little adjustment on the trail. These packs have four suspension points that make them pretty stable when you're hiking. They can "sweat-up" your back a bit. Carrying a shoulder pack may cause stiff shoulders until you get used to it.

A fanny pack is smaller and lighter and fits comfortably around your middle. It may need to be hitched up and tightened as you hike because it only rests on the hips as a single suspension point. Purchase a large fanny pack so you have enough room to carry all of your necessities. Be sure the fanny pack has a good belt with hip padding to protect you from abrasions.

The choice is up to you.

The Professor carries a new fanny pack made from recyclable materials. Badger Bob, no slave to fashion, relies on an old shoulder pack he has carried for the last twenty years. He has modified it a bit by adding an extra length of hip belt to encompass and secure his magnificence.

What should be in your pack? Foremost is **rain gear**. This could be a poncho, parka, or a full rain suit. There is a wide selection available. You could probably get by with a thirty-gallon trash bag with a head hole if you wanted, but it is not recommended. In Yellowstone, the weather can turn cool quickly, so you may need some extra warmth. A jacket or fleece can keep you warm.

WARNING, if the weather looks bad, don't go hiking. There are many other things to see and do in the Park until the weather is good. Fortunately, summer weather in Yellowstone is usually good.

Other items that should find their way into your pack include **_tissues and damp wipes._** Both items serve multiple purposes from toilet paper to nose wipes. Don't leave home without them. Take along a **_first aid kit_** and **_sun block_** (SPF 15 or greater). Be sure to use it before you go. Always take **_insect repellent_**. Bug bites are no fun. It's a good idea to leave itching and scratching to the Park animals.

Badger Bob takes a mosquito head net along. " If you only use the net once in your life, it will prove well worth the price you paid for it."

ALWAYS include a **_full water bottle_**, more if you drink a lot of water. Take **_trail snacks_** along. Homemade GORP (good old raisins, peanuts plus M&M's) works well. Other trail snacks are good too. Snacks will give you a lift when you need an energy boost.

Badger Bob carries beef jerky because he feels jerky gives him a longer lasting energy lift.

All hikes in this guide are on well-marked trails and the danger of getting lost is small. Still, it's a good idea to carry a good relief **_map_** of the hiking area and a compass for orientation.

Badger Bob always carries **_moleskin_** for blister protection. He will put one on at the FIRST sign of a hot spot or blister. Nothing will ruin a hike or vacation like a needless blister.

You are probably aware of what the sun can do, and probably has done to your skin and eyes. So, as well as sunscreen, take **_sunglasses_**. Wear a **_hat_** with a brim, and a back flap. This will protect your neck and ears. If funds are a problem, an old ball cap with a handkerchief covering your neck will do.

Another item you may want to add is a pair of trekking poles or **_hiking sticks_**. Call them your backcountry rod and staff. Trekking poles can reduce the wear and tear on your legs and knees by as much as fifteen percent. A Geezer knows this can be important! Trekking poles can also provide stability that may be lacking as one achieves age.

Badger Bob calls his trekking poles "pseudopods'" [false feet]. The Professor doesn't use poles on short, level hikes. On occasion he borrows the Badger's poles when extra support is needed to get just the right picture.

You are the best judge of your balance and the condition of your knees. If you enjoy trekking, these poles will become a valuable asset. If funds are a problem, buy a pair of used ski poles at the Salvation Army Store. They will do the job and save you money.

Black bear

A word about animals in Yellowstone: THESE ANIMALS ARE WILD. The Park is not a petting zoo. These animals are not Yogi Bear or Bobby Bison. They can be dangerous, especially, if the animal feels threatened or startled. Do not get too close. If you are lucky enough to see one of the "big four" (bear, moose, bison or elk) on the trail, slowly change your direction and move away. DO NOT TRY TO ATTRACT THE ANIMALS ATTENTION AND DO NOT RUN! Always give wild animals plenty of room. This photo of a black bear was taken with a long telephoto lens. A photo is never worth an injury.

This should cover the necessities. You may wish to carry other things in your pack like medications, makeup, market reports or a shovel. The options go on forever, but the choice is up to you.

The Professor carries maps, compass, plant identification books and field glasses in his pack, but it's all optional.

Medical conditions:

You and your doctor have a clear idea of your physical condition. Remember most hikes in the Park are above five thousand feet. Be informed and confident that your physical condition is good enough to hike in this country. Check with your doctor before hiking in Yellowstone, especially if you have any doubt about your physical abilities and safety.

Gneiss Creek Trail to Companula Creek.

This hike is in Yellowstone Park but is reached by a highway that does not pass through a Park gate. It's a good idea to have a Park pass, which you can pick up at any Park gate.

The trailhead is located on US 191 headed north out of West Yellowstone, Montana. Drive eight miles north and pass through the US 289 inter-section that goes west to Hebgen Lake. Don't turn here, it will do you no good. Keep driving north on 191 for a mile and a quarter [1 ¼]. Turn right [east] onto the dirt road at the Gneiss Creek Trailhead sign. The parking area is a small grassy pull-off. LOCK YOUR CAR AND TAKE YOUR KEYS WITH YOU. PUT THE KEYS IN A SECURE POCKET! MAKE SURE ONE OF YOUR HIKING PALS KNOWS WHERE A SPARE KEY IS LOCATED.

The Professor: "Rules and regulations are made for good reasons. They won't hurt you and they sure help the Park, so follow them – Thanks Partner!"

Badger Bob: "Losing your keys on the trail is a violation of the 'leave no trace' wilderness ethic. It's also expensive and irritating."

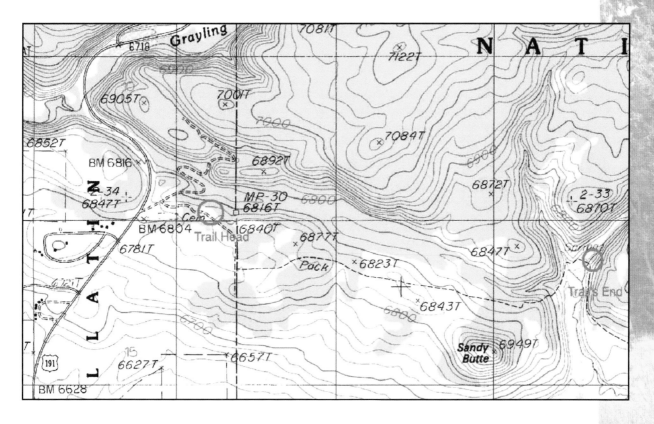

The Professor: "My geologist friends tell me gneiss is a kind of metamorphic rock with a funny pronunciation; gneiss sounds like 'nice' and rhymes with mice, — also dice and lice, but that's another story!"

The parking area is a woodland delight bounded by aspen and fir trees. There is a buck and rail fence to the south that marks the Yellowstone National Park boundary.

Get your gear and check it carefully. Take the trail heading east from the parking lot and let the fun begin.

Past the aspen grove (five minutes or so), you meet a huge leaning Douglas Fir tree. These large fellas can sometimes survive fires because they have thick bark. This is a pretty good defense mechanism against fire. But, as you will see later on the trail, it doesn't always work as well with large crown fires.

A bit further down the trail you will notice the markers that delineate the Yellowstone Park boundary. The trail parallels these markers. After ten minutes of hiking you'll reach the Gneiss Creek Trail Head. Take a farewell look at the houses back to the West and get ready for a walk on the wild side.

By now some new lady friends (mosquitoes) may be greeting you. It's a fact that all biting mosquitoes are females – imagine that! The males just suck plant nectar [what good guys!]. These buzzing babes may remind you it's time to put on the repellent. This will help keep these lovely ladies at arm's length. On the other hand, you've just had an experience with some of the really wild Yellowstone creatures.

It's great fun to stop and smell the roses. In this case, stop and sniff some of the amazing wild flowers that line the trail.

When Badger Bob passed this way in July, the fields were covered with different colored wildflowers. These colors and shapes will soon change.

Wildflowers bloom at different times in Yellowstone. The next plants to blossom will show new shapes and colors. This encourages a trekker to re-walk the trail just to see what's in bloom.

At the crest of a small rise, the Madison Valley comes into view to the south. This valley was burned in the 1988 fires and many trees were lost. The lodge-pole pines that now cover this valley are young and growing.

There was great concern that Yellowstone might be ruined by the '88 fires. The growth of these new trees shows the resiliency of the ecosystem. A great deal was learned about the role fire plays in Yellowstone.

On the other side of the hill you pass through a small Aspen stand. Interestingly, this tree cluster is considered one plant. Aspens propagate from underground runners. Technically, this grove of "trees" is one organism. So, what are sometimes called "trees" could be called clones.

The Badger sums it up succinctly, "Cool".

Beyond the aspen stand, the terrain changes dramatically. You've moved into a sagebrush meadow. The scientific name for this sagebrush is *Artemisia tridentata*. Its common name is big sagebrush.

Take a look at the leaves. They have three lobes or dents in the leaf. Just for fun, rub some of the sagebrush in your hands. Its pungent aroma reminds you of the kitchen herb. This wild sage relative won't do for cooking but it shares the sage name.

Mount Holmes in the distance

Badger Bob: "There's a really tough hike of about 12 miles that leads to the top of Mt. Holmes. This is NOT for the true Geezer who would like to be able to hike to the kitchen table the following morning."

By now you've been on the trail about thirty minutes. Topping a small rise, you will see an expanse of rolling hills extending east. In the far distance Mt. Holmes may be visible.

Are your toes tired at this point? Take a break – you've earned it. When you're on your feet and moving again, a waypoint comes in view.

Badger Bob calls these four isolated trees "The Four Aspens". [Very creative Bob!]

It's time for a Crazy Ivan (a 180° turn and view). Check out the mountains to the north-west. Awesome!

The trail takes a downward turn and you enter a stand of new growth lodgepole pines. These trees got their start after the 1988 fires. At twenty years of age these trees are six to eight feet tall and growing.

After an hour on the trail, you approach an old growth pine stand. One of the pines has two faded orange trail markers nailed to it at about head height (if you're on a horse). Look to the left at the lovely ravine leading down to Companula Creek. Here the trail drops rather steeply down to the creek bed.

This is a good turn around point for those who don't want to descend to the creek. It may not look too far down but remember you have to climb back up. Did you know 100 feet is about the same height as a five-story building? To climb back up the hill you need to have a little oomph left.

For those who made it down the hill, you're now in the valley of Companula Creek. There are lots of willows here to hide the moose. This is "Moose Munching Heaven," so keep a look out for these big boys.

Badger Bob's wife, a gorgeous gazelle, shares her philosophy "down is divine and level is lovely, but up can be ugly!". Badger Bob, purist at heart responds, "stop whining and start climbing". This night he dines alone.

On your way to Companula Creek you'll need to cross a couple of small run-off channels. Hop over them and head down to the creek. When you get to the running water it divides into two streams. The steams pass on both sides of a small island.

Each stream has its own half log bridge. Be careful crossing the second log bridge as it may feel a little "bouncy." This is a great spot to soak your toes, so drop your pack and spend a little time here!

This is also a good time to stop and smell the wild onions. They are easy to spot. They look like the onions you grow in your garden. You can look them up in your plant identification book. *Look up the short styled onion "Allium Brevistylum."*

Lewis Monkey Flower

The Professor: "While you are by the stream, look for the bright pink Lewis Monkey Flower (Mimulus lewisii). They grow close to the water. Look closely at the inflorescence [flower head]. You may see how it earned its name. The flower head supposedly looks like a little monkey's face. What do you think?"

Time to head back up, up, up the hill. Now you'll see why some folks stopped at the top! By the time you get up the hill, you'll be "panting like a panther." Take a moment and look back at Companula Creek. Take a deep whiff of backcountry air. It smells good doesn't it? Store this "out back" moment in your memory.

On the return trek notice how different things look than they did on the way in. "The Four Aspens" look completely different. Don't worry, you're not lost, you're on the way back to your ride!

From the sagebrush covered hill look down on civilization. It's all easy moving from here. Keep an eye peeled for mountain blue birds in the open meadow. The color of these little creatures will amaze you.

Welcome back to the trailhead. It has taken you about two hours. You have walked about four miles round trip. Congratulations! You're an Official Geezer Hiker. The merit badge is in the mail!

7

Bacon Rind Creek.

This hike is in Yellowstone Park but is reached by a highway that does not pass through a Park gate. It's a good idea to have a Park pass, which you can pick up at any Park gate.

To reach this trailhead drive north on US 191 out of West Yellowstone, Montana, for eighteen and one half [18 ½] miles. You will pass two trailheads on the east side of the road. The first trailhead on the **right** [east] is Big Horn Pass Trail. Two miles further on the **right** [east] is the Fawn Creek Trailhead.

Your goal is a side road one half [½] mile **past** Fawn Creek on the **left**, [west] side of the road. This is the access road for Bacon Rind Creek. The sign only says "**trailhead.**" It's easy to miss this one, so watch carefully.

Follow the access road to the parking area. Park your car and lock it. REMEMBER TO TAKE YOUR KEYS WITH YOU AND TELL A PAL WHERE A SPARE KEY IS LOCATED. Check your gear carefully. Slip on your pack and you are ready to go!

The Professor: "Park Rules and regulations are made for good reasons. They won't hurt you and they sure help the Park, so please follow them – Thanks, Partner!"

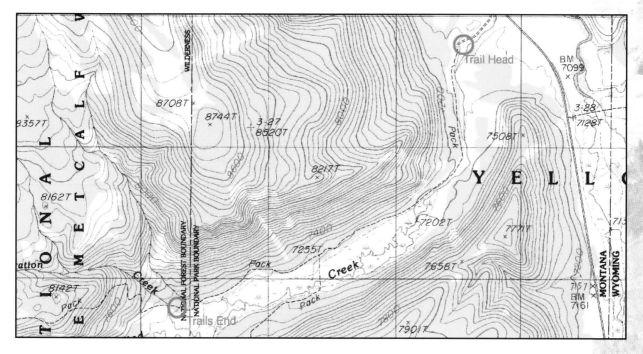

This is an easy hike all the way to the Park boundary. It's a pleasant walk through a sub-alpine canyon. The trail is lined with beautiful lodgepole pines and high canyon walls.

The trail begins by running parallel to Bacon Rind Creek. Soon the creek meanders off to the south while the trail stays on the north side of the canyon. Impressive walls rise steeply on either side of this gorgeous canyon. Notice the rock slides on both sides of the canyon.

Badger Bob spent some time pondering the huge freestanding rocks with trees growing out of them. Nothing was decided–except that nature is quite a gardener.

Take a gander at the large escarpment to the north. Beautiful!

It made Badger Bob feel small and humble [well maybe not].

While you're walking the trail, don't forget to look for animal signs, including scat, scratch, scent, rub, and tracks. It's fun to imagine what might have traveled the trail before you.

Badger Bob saw tree rubbing sites, where bison, elk or bear scratched their backs. The Professor thought he caught the scent of a large omnivore, but realized it was probably Badger Bob. The scat will be left to your imagination.

The canyon narrows as you move west. The meadow between the high canyon walls is increasingly covered with water loving willow thickets. Be sure to watch for moose. It's surprising how easily these huge animals can hide themselves in these short willow thickets , so keep a sharp eye! A mother moose protecting her baby can be dangerous!.

Moose

As Badger Bob strolled further along the trail he ran into some personal history from a previous hike in this valley.

Remember those free standing rocks out in the meadow? So does Badger Bob. He had been trying to identify the specie of a tree growing on top of one of these rocks. He decided he could get a better view by climbing to the top of the rock. Bad idea, Badger Bob.

Physics says "what goes up must come down" and so did Badger Bob. That's why he calls this Break Leg Rock. Why don't you look at the wild flowers at the base of Break Leg Rock and skip the fall from grace.

As you approach the Park boundary, the peaks of high mountains to the west become visible.

The most prominent peak is White Mountain. Imagine the amazing panoramic view from the top! You're getting close to the Yellowstone boundary where it meets the Lee Metcalf Wilderness. Not many folks have done a hike like this one.

Here a happy hiker (the Professor) shows his satisfaction with making the grade. He's probably wondering, "How many Olympic Marathoners have done this hike?"

After about an hour of hiking and sightseeing, the red and white markers of the Park boundary come into view.

The next somewhat obvious marker is the rustic sign announcing the Lee Metcalf Wilderness.

12

Why not walk the boundary and look for day-beds where animals have rested in the meadow? Day beds are used by animals as cool, soft, snoozing spots. Most day beds are vacated by the time you arrive. The signs tell you someone was home earlier. Look around, you can find a day bed too!

This is a typical daybed. Something was resting here, but what?

It's time to head west, past the boundary markers toward a small run-off creek. Can you find the log bridge? Did you spot the lone aspen?

Badger Bob and the Professor crossed the log bridge to a shady resting spot. Badger Bob took a short nap under a lodgepole. Even Badger Bob needs rest!

This is a good turn around point. The trail you have been hiking now climbs steeply up and out of the canyon.

As you head "back to the future," be sure to pull a Crazy Ivan (180° turn and view) at the old trail marker just outside the Park boundary. It's nice to see where you've been because that was where you were going.

Now you're back at the willow flats. Do another Crazy Ivan.

Who can get enough of that view?

Remember this spot? You're almost to the trailhead. Keep on truckin'.

The end is in sight. It's a good time to file this hike away in your memory. Save it for a future camp-fire tale.

Badger Bob believes trekkers should visit the ice cream shop after hiking. Moose Tracks ice cream is a real treat. It's a good life.

Mary Mt. Trail to the Nez Perce Bridge

There are two routes to this trailhead – one from West Yellowstone, MT via Madison Junction, and the other from Old Faithful.

Starting at the West Entrance to Yellowstone Park, drive east to Madison Junction. Turn right toward Old Faithful on the Grand Loop Road. Drive six [6] miles south from Madison Junction, (nineteen [19] miles from the West Entrance). Turn left [east] into the parking area for the Mary Mountain Trail. Alternatively, starting at Old Faithful, drive west nine [9] miles on the grand loop road. Turn right [east] into the Mary Mountain parking area.

Park the car and check your gear. SECURE YOUR KEYS, AND SHOW A PAL WHERE YOU KEEP A SPARE KEY. It's a real drag to return from a hike and find you're locked out of the car.

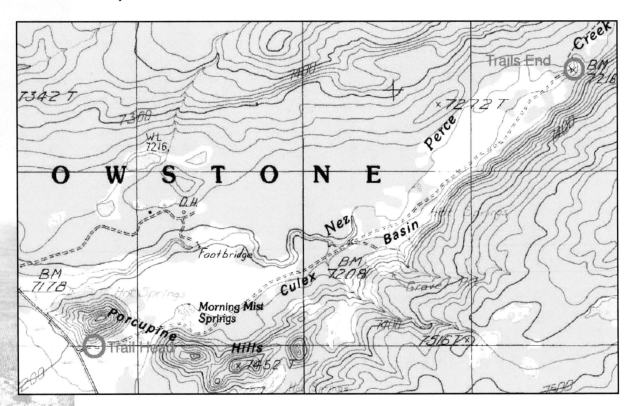

Although the sign at the trailhead says "Mary Mountain – 11 miles," pay it no mind. You will be turning back at the old bridge over Nez Perce Creek. This is only two [2] miles east of the trailhead where your hike begins.

Adjust your pack and head east on the old abandoned service road. This wide path makes it easy for two hikers to walk side by side and chat.

The Professor: "A good rule of thumb for hiking speed is this: if you're walking too fast to talk comfortably, slow down, you're walking too fast."

Since this is a former service road, you may see relics along the trail. These historical remnants are cultural artifacts and part of Yellowstone history. These items should not to be moved or removed. It is interesting to look at these items and try to figure out how they were used.

Badger Bob climbed the northern hill and found the top covered with elk droppings. "I guess it's an elk lookout. Maybe elk like the high ground so they can see what may be trying to sneak up on them," Bob explains.

As you pass between two small hills, the view opens and you enter the first meadow of the Culex Basin.

Past the hills the visual change is abrupt. You are entering a region of thermal activity with steaming hot pools. There are no boardwalks here, so for your personal safety use good sense.

Watch yourself because these areas can be dangerous. Thin crusts near thermal features may not support your weight and you could break through and be badly burned or worse.

Soon you are hiking through buffalo habitat. On this trail the large creatures leave behind signs of their migration. Look for hoof prints, hair, and droppings on the path. Keep an eye out for these big animals as well.

A number of bison winter on the western side of the Park where they can seek warmth from thermal features. When spring arrives, many of these animals migrate over Mary Mountain to the eastern side of the Park. Some bison spend the summer in the Hayden Valley. The bison usually calve in May.

Bison and calf

In late summer the buffalo enter the rut [romance bison style]. Following the rut the animals migrate back to the western side of the Park. The process repeats itself from season to season.

The Professor: "These beasts are fast and unpredictable, so if you encounter one on the trail, give it a wide berth and the respect it's due. This means not approaching, vocalizing, or harassing the animal. You may have to move off the trail or turn back. Otherwise, you may really get the point."

After migration, the Mary Mountain trail contains considerable signs of the bison's passing. In some places the trail is so wide and well trodden it resembles a "bison superhighway." When passing through the trees on this trail, look for tree rubs. Can you spot any left over hair from the winter coats bison shed as they migrate?

Soon the trail alternates between stands of lodgepole pine and the open meadows of Culex Basin. [What's a culex? It's a mosquito, of course!]

In Yellowstone it's common to see downed pines. Although these trees are adapted to the soil here, some of them can't withstand a strong windstorm. This is because of the relatively small root system and the shallow soil in the Culex Basin.

Check out the root system on one of these fallen trees. You'll notice there are no taproots. Here the soil is so thin there is very little to tap!

On both sides of the trail Badger Bob observed several thermal features he had not seen before. He wondered if the features were new or if he had just not noticed them previously.

What a really cool surprise! (Well, OK, hot).

The visual effect is superb. Where else in the world could you see something like this? Plus, there are no folks on a boardwalk to obstruct your view.

Shortly after passing these thermal features, notice a red cliff on the south side of the trail. Does this look natural or did man cause this? Hint: Look for 'Gravel Pit' on the map.

Look closely at the big rocks below the cliff face. Can you find the tool and drill marks on some of the larger rocks?

What went on here? When did this occur? Who was in charge? Why did this happen? These are good questions.

The Professor: "It's time to head to the Park library in Mammoth to find the answers."

In several places the trail overlooks meandering Nez Perce Creek. The creek was named after the famous Indian tribe.

The Professor: "This is another great opportunity to visit the Park library at Mammoth and read the whole story of chief Joseph, the Nez Perce and their flight through Yellowstone."

Forty minutes into the hike, you'll encounter a small hot pot that has taken over the trail. This beautiful little pool displays all the characteristics of its larger brothers at better-known locations.

The Professor pointed out that multicolored bacterial growths indicate water temperature variations as the water emerges from the pool. The light gray color is where there is limited growth due to extreme temperatures. The colors change from light yellow, to darker yellow, and finally orange as the water cools. Proteins isolated from these bacteria have proven to be very useful in biotechnology and medical science. Badger Bob made what he deemed an appropriate comment: "Huh?"

21

This raven keeps a wary eye on Nez Perce Creek.

After about an hour on the trail you'll reach the old footbridge over Nez Perce Creek.

Here Badger Bob boards the broken bridge to look for cut-throat trout. The clever trout could be hiding under the bridge. Badger Bob has no luck in spotting the wily swimmers. Too bad Bob, but you couldn't keep 'em if you caught 'em anyway. This is a catch and release stream.

This is a great place to drop your pack and have a snack. Some folks may want to cross the bridge and continue up the creek (no pun intended!). The trail continues to skirt Nez Perce Creek for the next mile or so where a large rockslide nearly blocks the trail. It's a great place to look for picas, [little rock rabbits]. If you continue on this way keep an eye out for the little fellows.

For those hikers whose goal is the bridge, this is your turn around point. Take your time and enjoy yourself. Soon it's time to head back down the trail to your vehicle. When you reach the car stow your gear. Now break out the cooler for a bite and a beverage. It's been a great hike, but all trekkers need to rest up and stoke up for the next hike.

Felicitations, friends!

A pica peeks from the rocks.

Sentinel Meadows

There are two ways to reach this trailhead: one from the West Park entrance at Yellowstone West, Montana, via Madison junction and the other from Old Faithful traveling west toward Madison junction.

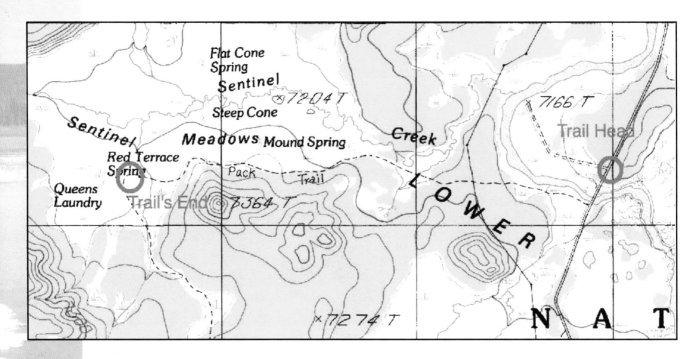

From the West Entrance, head east to Madison Junction. Turn right [south] at the junction and head toward Old Faithful. Take the Fountain Flats exit on the right [west], five and one half [5 ½] miles from Madison junction (seventeen [17] miles from the West Entrance). Alternatively, from Old Faithful drive west on the grand loop road ten [10] miles. Take the Fountain Flats exit on the left [west].

Follow the access road to the parking area. Lock your car. SECURE YOUR KEYS AND SHOW A FELLOW HIKER WHERE TO LOCATE A SPARE KEY. Remember, it's a long way to a locksmith. Check your gear and get ready to go.

There were several visitors at the trailhead and Badger Bob wondered, "Where do all these folks come from?" Realizing there was no clear answer, the Professor offered no comment.

This trail begins on a bicycle path that used to be part of the old Fountain Flats Freight Road.

Badger Bob heads south down the trail in search of Ojo Caliente.

Ojo Caliente Hot Spring appears on your right [west] before you reach the trailhead. This is a bonus feature. Get a close up look and maybe a photo at Ojo.

Head south across the Firehole River Bridge. Just across the trail, turn right [west] onto the Sentinel Meadows trail.

Follow the trail along the river. Soon it reaches a double half-log bridge. This bridge keeps your boots dry while crossing Fairy Creek. This small stream runs into the Fire Hole River.

After crossing the bridge there's a good view of the '88 fire effects and the new growth that has occurred since then.

Most of the downed trees you see along the way are fire casualties. These pictures were taken in 2008 and the new lodge pole pines sprouted after the '88 fires have reached about 8-10 feet in height.

Further down the trail a series of power lines cuts the horizon:

The power lines caused the Professor to stop and pontificate on the cost/lost-benefits of marring the natural beauty with human improvements. After walking under the power lines, the beautiful vista reopened and the Professor's protestations were soon forgotten.

Several thermal areas are visible on the horizon. To the north, lodgepole pines line Sentinel Creek. It's worth a side trip for a look-see.

Badger Bob and the Professor spotted a bison bull standing near the stream. The old boy seemed at peace with the world, so the pair of hikers avoided him. They hoped the old buffalo would remain at peace, especially with them.

Near the stream more bison sign became apparent. Buffalo chips abounded. Interestingly, there were several wallowed out low spots. Rolling buffalo made these sandy depressions.

The trail is clear and easy to follow. It's interesting and helpful to teach yourself to watch for trail indicators other than the trodden path. Look for cut logs, orange tags and other trail signs. These indicators assure you that you are on the right track.

After walking for about 40 minutes, you will spot an easily identifiable waypoint. You've arrived at campsite OG1. This is a beautiful spot for overnight camping.

Soon you top a small rise. Here you can pull a Crazy Ivan [180° turn and view]. You are looking at an American wilderness with no sign of human improvements. It might occur to you that nature is indeed a great engineer!

The wild flowers are in bloom in July and the sweet smells that waft on the breeze may lift your spirits. At this time of year, the trail is lined with sulfur buckwheat *(Eriogonum umbellatum)*, snow-colored yarrow *(Achillea millefollium)* and a myriad of other beautiful wild flowers.

Don't forget to watch for wild birds. The '88 fires have made new habitat for mountain birds. In this area blue birds abound.

The trees and blue birds are soon left behind and thermal features once again capture your wandering gaze. There are lots more features to see as you follow this trail.

Here Badger Bob bows to the lupines, or could it be the old sniff test?

Only the Badger knows for sure.

What captures your attention? Could it be thermals, open country, tree lines, animal signs, or the horizon?

Red Terrace Spring
and a buffalo wallow
come into view.

Soon several thermal
features are in sight.
The larger mound is
called Steep Cone.

These thermal features
are impressive.

Here, the open
vistas make hiking
through a burn
area much more
interesting.

Soon the hike brings you around to the west side of the hill. Several large pines invite you to take a break in the shade.

While Badger Bob was power napping, the Professor was scanning the horizon for something of interest.

The Professor spotted a thermal feature with a man made structure near it. These points of interest are about five hundred yards to the west.

The structure looks like a log cabin minus the roof. The thermal feature appears to be a hot spring.

Good job Professor! You have spotted what is believed to be the first public building ever constructed in Yellowstone Park.

It was, or is, an unfinished bathhouse started in 1881 by the Park's second Superintendent, Philitus W. Norris. Norris was replaced before the bathhouse was finished, but the structure still stands. The bathhouse has been preserved by soaking up mineral-laden thermal water. The source of run-off water preserving the bathhouse comes from a thermal pool called The Queens Laundry Spring.

It's difficult to imagine how anyone could "bathe" or do laundry in these scalding waters. But, it has been reported that early Park visitors did both. These activities are no longer permitted in this fragile area.

The trail continues and wanders through areas much like those you have just hiked. This is a good turn around spot.

Badger Bob: "Great hike! Just turn around and retrace your steps back to the parking area. Please pick up any trash that some inexperienced trail hand or thoughtless hiker may have dropped. The next trekker will have a better experience all because of your effort. Thank you."

As you are headed back to your ride, you may be thinking of an ice chest full of cool beverages and tempting snacks. You may want to check your camera so the next photo opportunity won't be a flop. The Professor grins, knowing such events will never befall him [again].

Sunshine and blue skies to you.

The Lewis River Channel

There are two routes to reach this trailhead. One is north bound from the south Park entrance, and the other is south bound from Grant Village.

To reach the trailhead from the south entry gate, follow the grand loop road twelve [12] miles north. Look on the left [west] side of the road for the Lewis Channel trailhead marker and the Dogshead hiking trail.

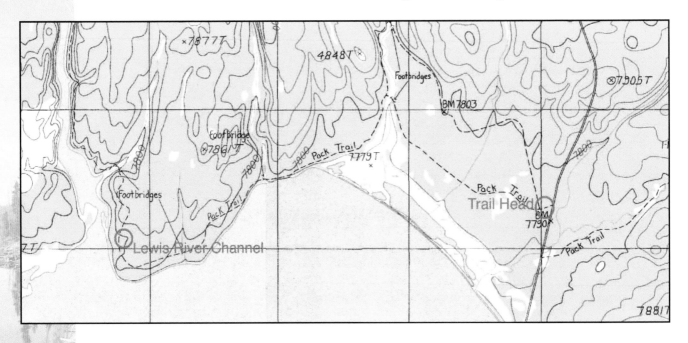

To reach the trailhead from Grant village, follow the grand loop road five [5] miles south and look for the trailhead on the right [west] side of the road.

Badger Bob considers his options. Take the left fork for Lewis Channel, Badger Bob!

*There are two trailheads within several yards of each other. Badger Bob and the Professor should take the **LEFT** trailhead [southern one], **NOT** the trailhead on the right.*

Check your gear. Lock your car. SECURE YOUR KEYS AND MAKE SURE SOMEONE HAS A SPARE KEY.

It's time to hike the Lewis River Channel trail with a light heart and a smile. Don't forget your camera. The photographic opportunities on this trip are immense.

On this hike you will meet, greet, and walk through mixed forests, (both old and new growth).

The trek goes through moist areas as well as forest land, so be prepared. There may be "Lots of Ladies" [mosquitoes] present. Be sure to take your REPELLENT!

F.Y.I.: Some folks can't tell a fir tree from a spruce tree, but you can. Here's how: Shake hands with the tree [get the feel of it]. Fir trees have flat friendly needles that feel nice to the touch. Spruce trees have sharp, sticky needles that are scratchy to touch. Now you know!

During the summer this path is bounded by lush grass and ground-covering plants. The trail is lined with grouse whortleberry, *(Vaccinium scoparium)*. The locals call this plant dwarf huckleberry. The pea sized, red berries are sweet and very tasty. The bears *[and Badger Bob]* love them.

Beside the trail you may see moist areas where a special plant grows. Look for numerous pink blossoms on a tall upright stem. Take a closer look at one of the blooms. It looks like a pink elephant's trunk. That's why it's called Elephant Head *(Pedicularis groenlandica)*. If there has been a heavy winter snow runoff or plenty of rain, there will be lots of Elephant Head.

Grouse Whortleberry

Elephant Head

This area experienced a burn in the 1988 fires and there are many burned tree trunks still standing. These stumps are dead wood and can be blown down by the wind. Watch out for possible deadfalls [trees that can fall without warning].

Soon the trail will bring you to an open meadow. The Professor smiled, and told Badger Bob that he was reminded of the first time he had gone to Shoshone Lake back in July of 1963. The Professor claimed to have run the entire way, just to avoid the "ladies". Badger Bob made a sound that was less than kind.

Do you remember your tutorial on how to recognize the differences between fir and spruce trees? The Professor hopes so, because it's time to put that knowledge to the test while you are moving through spruce and fir stands.

The trail leads you into a stand of old growth lodgepole pines. Watch your step. There are roots and rocks on the trail to trip you.

The trees in this area will give you a picture of how woodland trails looked before the fires of 1988.

On this hike you may encounter some downed trees on the trail. Step over them and keep on hiking.

Badger Bob crossed the channel and points the way with his Pseudopod [trekking pole].

Twenty-five minutes into the hike, the trail crosses a Lewis Lake run-off channel.

The trail now parallels the run-off channel and heads south toward Lewis Lake.

Thirty minutes on the trail brings you to a footbridge. This will be a familiar landmark on your return trip.

Lewis Lake was named after Meriweather Lewis. He was one of the leaders of the Lewis and Clark expedition. Lewis was also an amateur botanist. The Lewis Monkey flower is named in honor of him.

The Professor said that Meriweather Lewis was a truly interesting individual, and Badger Bob agreed.

It's a short walk to Lewis Lake. When you arrive you will be ready for a lakeside experience.

Check out the mountainous views. Soon you will pass what looks like a grass covered park area. Actually it's a marsh filled with pond lilies. These plants live both over and under the water. Although this looks like a golf course, don't go for a walk here or you may find yourself wading.

Just a few steps further and you can see Lewis Lake. There is no wind on this clear morning and the lake is very quiet. Not a ripple on its surface.

Remember this calm event because things can change quickly in Yellowstone.

Lewis Lake is diamond clear. Nothing is moving. The sand on the beach is black. This black sand is the color of the obsidian that is created in volcanic eruptions.

The water at the beach is warm, but cools rapidly as you move away from the bank.

Keep your feet dry, Badger Bob.

Badger Bob heard the call of a
loon by the lake and the Professor
spotted a bald eagle flying overhead
– a great bonus on a great hike.

Here the life cycle of the forest is in full evidence. Old trees have died, young trees are growing, and trees that have fallen into the lake have been blown back up on shore, washed clean of their bark and dried in the sun. Hard to believe the landscape is this beautiful, but it is!

The Professor told Badger Bob that he was quite proud of his photos. He bragged on his Brownie Hawkeye camera that has held up so well over the years. [Right, Professor!]

Lewis Lake is unbelievably clear and the shoreline draws your attention south to the Grand Teton Mountains.

Now the trail rises and takes you above the lake. Soon you'll re-enter the pine forest.

It's time for a little uphill walking.

Before you know it, you reach an overview of the Lewis River Channel that links Lewis Lake to Shoshone Lake.

Look for canoes and flatbottom boats across the channel. If you are so inclined, you can rent one of these watercraft and further your trip up the creek [pun intended].

Kudos! You have arrived at your destination and turn-around point. Take a well-deserved break. Drop your pack, sit down, have a beverage and something to munch on while you absorb the view.

Here is a rhyme from the Professor for your break:

An Ode to Bear Scat on the Trail

Seeing bear scat when it's old

Is GREAT and proves they're here.

But seeing bear scat when it's fresh,

I worry they're too near!

Badger Bob indulges himself (again) with water and trail mix. Bob also enjoys a breeze off the lake.

A short walk east brings you back to open water. Notice the different mood of Lewis Lake now. It was dead calm on the lake this morning.

Things can change quickly in Yellowstone, but it's time for another little break on the way back to the trailhead.

Stop to smell the flowers – No, wait! This is not a flower! These are the leaves of the Scarlet Paintbrush (*Castilleja miniata*).

Scarlet Paintbrush

Ready for another break to catch your breath? Why not stop and count the tree rings on one of the large sawed logs along the trail. Each of the rings shows a year's growth. Some of these large trees were alive and well when Lewis and Clark were here.

Remember this bridge? The Professor casts a long shadow. You are almost to your rig.

Badger Bob heads back across the run-off channel, then welcome back to the trailhead and "Cheers, Mate!

Are you ready for the next hike?

Riddle Lake

There are two ways to reach the Riddle Lake trailhead: one from the South Entrance on the grand loop road headed north, and the other from the Grant Village intersection on the grand loop road headed south.

To reach the trailhead from Grant Village, turn south [left] at the intersection of Grant Village and Grand Loop road. Drive south three [3] miles. Pull into the Riddle Lake trailhead on the left [east] side of the highway. To reach the trailhead from the South Entrance, drive north sixteen [16] miles. Pull into the Riddle Lake trailhead on the right [east] side of the road.

Get your gear, lock your car, and get ready to go.

DON'T FORGET YOUR KEYS AND BE SURE TO SHOW A PAL WHERE YOU KEEP A SPARE KEY.

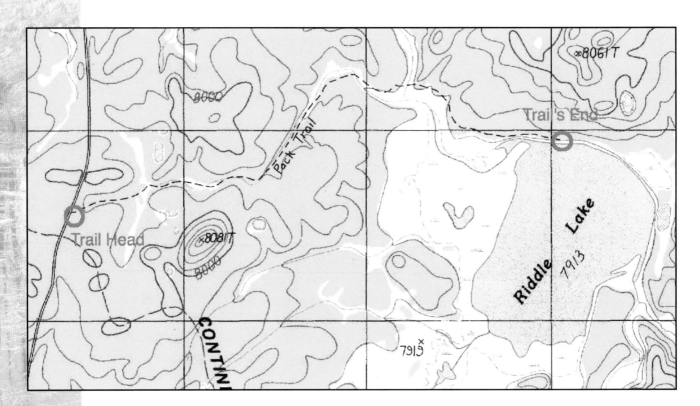

This is a hike through the woods to a beautiful backcountry lake. The whole family can take this trek together. As a bonus, this walk will help everyone feel comfortable about hiking in the backcountry.

Badger Bob and the Professor met three families of hikers during the first few minutes of the walk.

Begin this hike along the easily followed trail. The path winds through stands of lodge pole pine [old and new growth] on the way to the lake.

You are sure to enjoy the changing scenery of open forest, meadows, and wetlands. Each of these areas has different variations of vegetation. Notice the different species, colors, shapes and smells of the plant life.

The old growth reminded the Professor of what the forest looked like before the fires of 1988. The new growth tells the tale of recovery and new beginnings. It's a great feeling to know Mother Nature met the conflagration with a good working plan.

Badger Bob remembered taking this hike with Mrs. Badger back in the 1960's. Fishing in Riddle Lake was allowed at that time. As Badger Bob tells the story, Riddle Lake was where Mrs. Badger caught her first trout. Badger Bob, good husband that he was, promptly ate her trout for supper. True love knows no bounds.

You may see the occasional pile of pinecone scales on the side of the trail. Do you wonder how this pile of discarded pinecone parts came to be here? Could it be an animal feast or something else at work? To answer this question and other puzzles in Yellowstone, contact the Yellowstone Association. This organization offers classes led by highly educated professionals who know the how, when, why and where of the Yellowstone ecosystem.

The Professor recommends that anyone interested in Yellowstone Park history or natural events should contact the Yellowstone Association. Visitors are encouraged to inquire about the courses and join the Association. You can reach the Association at www.YellowstoneAssociation.org. Badger Bob solved the pinecone mystery by pointing out the mess was probably caused by a squirrel.

Along this beautiful trail you will see fir, spruce and pine trees. Compare the differences among them. This is also a great time to take out your plant identification book and put it to good use.

Kneel down, catch your breath and identify an interesting woodland flower or plant along the way.

Badger Bob examines the dry run-off channel that parallels the trail.

Green Gentian

The Professor posed a question:

"What is this tall green plant? Do you know anything about it?" Badger Bob frowned but looked up Green Gentian (Frasera speciosa) in his wildflower book. Bob admitted that it did have a cool scientific name and an odd growth cycle. " Why this plant could be as old as me!" Thank you, Badger Bob.

Leaving the woods and topping a small rise, rewards you with your first glimpse of the mountains to the south.

These are the Red mountains. If you have field glasses, see if you can spot the lookout tower on top of the tallest mountain peak. You're looking at Mount Sheridan!

Also from this viewpoint you can see the west side of Riddle Lake. The water is covered with Indian pond lilies *(Nuphar polysepalum)*. During the summertime, the beautiful yellow flowers of this plant are seen on top of the water.

Moving east along the trail, your view of the lake changes. Soon you will be able to see open water and burned timber on the east bank.

The pond lilies look like a green field of plants with bright yellow flowers. You might think you could walk on them. Don't try it without waders or a boat.

Soon you arrive at the beach. Pick out a nice log to sit on and break out the beverages and munchies.

Lookout tower

Across the lake you can see the Red Mountains again from a different viewpoint. If you look closely, you may be able to see the lookout tower on Mount Sheridan even without field glasses.

It's a great time to relax and get into the Zen of the scenery. Why not kick back and enjoy yourself?

Snack time, rest time, and view time is about over. It's time to retrace your tracks back to your ride. Store the good memories for a rainy day.

This is one of the more popular backcountry hikes in Yellowstone. It's also a great introduction to back country hiking. There are more and different hikes to take in the future. It's time to get your mind ready for another trek. Tally-ho!

Storm Point

This trailhead is easy to find. Take the East Entrance road at the Fishing Bridge intersection. Drive east four and a half [4 ½] miles. Turn right [south] into the Indian Pond and Storm Point parking area.

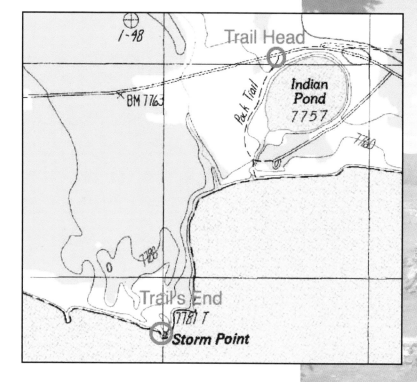

Park and be impressed with Indian Pond. There is much more to this feature than meets the eye. Before you start your hike, read the sign board about Indian Pond. This is truly an explosive story.

Check your gear. Have your camera primed and ready to shoot. Lock your car. BE SURE YOUR KEYS ARE WITH YOU AND SECURE. TELL A FRIEND WHERE YOU KEEP A SPARE KEY.

Badger Bob reads the story board at Indian pond. Even Bob is absorbed. [perhaps self-absorbed?]

Take some pictures of Indian pond before you start your hike.

Examine the plant life near the trailhead. The wildflowers are astounding. You will probably stop and smell the flowers more than once.

There is a great story about one of these flowers. It's called cinquefoil *(Potentilla Arguta)*. This attractive plant has small bright yellow blossoms and is plentiful all over the mountain west.

The interesting thing about cinquefoil is its leaves resemble the leaves of the marijuana plant. You may remember in the 1960's young people were smoking large amounts of marijuana, which was a considerable problem for law enforcement.

A story got out that cinquefoil had drug properties similar to

marijuana. Some folks said they were getting high from smoking it. Since cinquefoil is plentiful in the mountain west, law enforcement people were apprehensive because of the daunting task of trying to remove it from the countryside.

After some investigation, it turned out the stories were untrue. There were no mind-altering chemicals in cinquefoil. This spared law enforcement a ton of work and rescued a bunch of wonderful wildflowers for you to view [plus a great story to share].

Cinquefoil

Onward and outward. The trail heads south and runs parallel to the shore of Indian Pond. Look for waterfowl as you pass this spectacular body of water.

As you walk through the meadow you will come to a fork in the trail. Stay on the left fork of the trail. The right fork is the return path for this loop hike.

Most hikes close to human activity reduce the chances of seeing large animals in Yellowstone Park.

Bear in mind, [pun intended] you can see almost any animal that lives here almost any time and anywhere.

Badger Bob was once surprised when he and some hiking pals encountered a chubby cinnamon-colored black bear. This portly lady was walking near the two pines on the north shore of the lake. The old girl simply ignored the hikers and continued on her way. The hikers in Bob's party had all chosen the better part of valor. They had wisely visited the nearby forest. "This is a busy place," said Badger Bob stepping out from behind a tree.

There is a great view of Yellowstone Lake from this meadow. This huge lake is very cold and boaters must be careful not to fall in. Exposure to its cold temperature will cause hypothermia in a matter of minutes.

Cinnamon-colored Black Bear

Enjoy the panoramic views from the south shoreline of Yellowstone Lake. The large, open vista with the Absaroka Mountains lining the background is breathtaking.

The trail continues around the bay. Abruptly, it drops down into a drainage channel that can be crossed via the sturdy footbridge.

The water in this channel looks like iced tea. What causes this? Could it be tannins from the timbers floating in the water? Does the color come from elements in the soil?

Badger Bob asked the Professor if he knew the reason for the waters color. The Professor was silent, suggesting less erudition than might have been expected given his appellation.

Cross over the bridge and climb the bank on the other side. Now you're in for a great walk in a old growth pine forest. Take in another wonderful view of Lake Yellowstone.

The forest here was spared from the 1988 fires. This woodland area resembles Yellowstone Park the world knew before the '88 fires.

Use your senses in the old forest and take a big sniff of the woodland odors around you. Enjoy the great smells of the big Douglas fir trees and the sweet scent of the woodland wildflowers. There may also be some less pleasant odors. Simply ignore them.

You are now moving along the lakeshore beneath the trees. Keep your eyes open for the unexpected.

Badger Bob and the Professor spotted two river otters (Lutra canadensis) swimming in Mary Bay. The otters were very close to the shore. They were performing water acrobatics around the floating and partially submerged logs. The Professor had his camera with him and was shooting pictures. Sadly, he did not get a good picture of the two swimmers. It really didn't matter because this unexpected otter encounter was another high point of the hike.

The hike takes you up a slight grade. Why not take a break and look up a wild flower in your plant guide. Some hikers would rather sit on a log and rest a bit. The choice is yours.

Up and at 'em. Before you know it you've topped the hill. Now you enter an open meadow.

Notice the low spots on either side of the trail. In some of these low areas there are warm places caused by thermal heat close to the surface. The bison sometimes use these "hot spots" in the wintertime to help combat the cold.

You've been hiking for about thirty minutes. Storm Point is in sight. It's due south on the trail. The point is already impressive and you haven't even arrived.

Yellowbelly Marmot

Notice the pile of rocks to the right of the trail. This rock pile is sometimes home to yellowbelly marmots *(Marmota flaviventris)*. These furry critters are part of the squirrel family *(Sciuridae)*. Hike out to Storm Point and you will find proof under your feet that marmots have been here before you. As you pass the rock pile take a look and see if any impressive wildflowers are in bloom.

When Badger Bob and the Professor passed here there was golden colored sulfur buckwheat *(Eriogonum umbellatum)* in profusion.

Sulfur Buckwheat

Now you're on the way to the tip of Storm Point. The overview of Lake Yellowstone is amazing.

Look west young man! Notice how the loop trail parallels the southern shore of the lake. After several hundred yards the trail turns north. The remainder of the trail leads you through thick woodlands and back to the parking area.

You have reached the destination of your hike. Take some mental pictures and store them away to share with friends later.

A 180° turn and view gives you a wonderful panorama of Mary Bay.

Now it's decision time. Storm Point is the midway point of your trek. You can complete the loop hike or return the way you came.

Badger Bob and the Professor elect to return the way they entered. They hoped to see the two otters again to get a good photo. The two otters were not seen again by the two hopeful geezer gazers. Such is life and luck.

Here is the bridge, a familiar waypoint.

Badger Bob is back in the trees.

Badger Bob walks the footbridge.

Remember the two pines? *(a very beary spot)*

Welcome back to the trailhead.

Storm Point is one of the most popular hikes in Yellowstone Park. Now you can see why.

This might be a good time to stop at the Fishing Bridge store and try some Moose Tracks ice cream.

Bottoms up!

Hike Eight –

Wapiti Lake Trail, via Ribbon Lake Trail to Artist Point

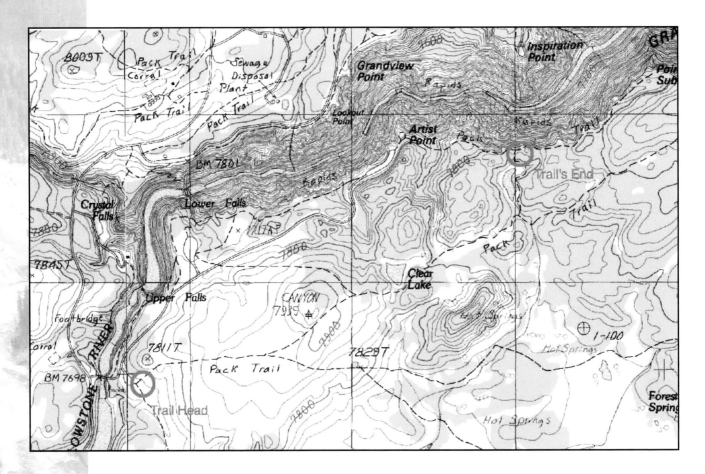

The best way to reach this trailhead is from Canyon Village. Drive One [1] mile [south] toward Lake, from the intersection of Canyon Village and the Norris road. Take a left [west] on the Artist Point access road. Take another quick right [south] into the parking area just past the Chittenden bridge on the right [south] side of the road. The Chittenden Bridge spans the Yellowstone River. The view is awesome and should get your adrenaline flowing. The trailhead has a spacious concrete parking facility with restrooms and a picnic area. The trailhead is east of the parking spaces.

This hike requires a little more physical effort than others, but it's well worth the effort. Lock your car and check your gear. Don't forget the water bottle, bug spray, camera, sunscreen and sunglasses.

SECURE YOUR KEYS AND TELL A PAL WHERE YOU KEEP A SPARE KEY.

If you're ready, put on your pack and head for the trail.

Badger Bob ponders his options.

The trail to Artist Point takes you through grass and sagebrush country. This is an area where bison graze and hang out. You are almost sure to see some of these large beasts. Remember to keep your distance.

The buffalo may look easy going but that can change in an instant, especially if the animal feels threatened. The bison is huge, fast and can be extremely dangerous. Give him a wide berth and let him take any path he chooses, anytime he wants.

Badger Bob heads east on the Wapiti Lake trail. Wapiti is another name for Elk. We didn't see any on this hike, but you're sure to see them somewhere in the park!

Bison

The professor: "Remember, he who gives the bison his way, will live to hike another day".

Elk

The view changes as you crest the hill. You can see a portion of the Grand Canyon of the Yellowstone to the north. The valley of Sour Creek is in front of you and to the east.

Look for the watering holes where the bison stop to drink.

There may even be some of these large beasts having a beverage as you view the area.

The trail leads down the hill into the trees and through some interesting thermal features.

Did Badger Bob check the rain gear?

There is always a chance of a rain shower in Yellowstone. Being wet and cold in the backcountry is **not** a good thing. Your rain gear should always be in your pack and readily available.

Badger Bob and The Professor believe you should always take your pack along. The Professor has a test for you. See how you do on the test.

This is a multiple-choice test. Remember you must select the correct answer(s).

Anyone who doesn't take his pack along is :

    [a] a bad Apple
    [b] a dumb Bunny
    [c] a Cock-eyed optimist
    [d] a Dumb fool
    [e] Each of the above

And the correct answer is: [F] **always take your pack along.**

🎵 Down in the valley where the buffalo roam.

Soon you reach a divide in the trail. The right fork continues on to Wapiti Lake, while the left fork heads to Clear Lake and Artist Point.

Take the left fork.

Badger Bob and the Professor spotted a large group of hikers following them on the trail. The two geezers met this group on their return trip from Artist Point. The groups destination was also Artist Point.

These fine folks came from France so the conversation was somewhat limited — they couldn't seem to understand the Professor's German. Who knew?

Thirty minutes into the hike you crest a rise and look down into the Sour Creek valley.

Badger Bob checks out a buffalo rub where the trail enters the timber.

Badger Bob explained to the Professor that this species of deer are called Mule deer. Then, Bob asked the Professor "Can you guess why?

The Professor just sighed.

The Professor spotted a young Mule deer near the trail.

A short walk down the path and a different landscape greets you. Welcome to a thermal area complete with the sights, sounds and smells that accompany it.

Did you get a big whiff of Clear Lake? Can you see its surface bubbling? Can you hear the lake gurgling? Didn't Will Shakespeare write about some witches who would probably feel right at home here?

Do you think the bubbles are the source of the smell?

The Professor mused that "Clear" Lake was definitely a misnomer.

It was Badger Bob's turn to sigh.

Badger Bob is impressed. "Why, this looks like a different planet!"

Not to be out done by the knowledgeable Professor; Badger Bob quoted his own adage: "The worse the smell the better the thermal feature." BB

Trail markers are sometimes bleached white – but they still point to where you want to go.

As you visit this unsettling area the shapes and views keep changing.

It isn't long until you pass a pair of large active mud pots. Keep to the right and don't get too close to take photos. These boys can spit in your eye from a distance!

A danger sign is posted in the thermal basin. The Park Service means it. Please stay on the trail.

Experts with years of experience make the park regulations. These rules are made to protect you and the park. Please follow them.

It's decision time. Cheers to those of you who have made it this far. You've done a great job, but from here to Artist Point there is a considerable amount of **UP.**

The visual is awesome and worth the effort to get there. BUT, some folks may have hiked far enough.

Do not overtax your body. If you are even a little spent, or if you feel that you have had enough, it is time to turn back.

Lily Pad Pond (unnamed on the map) offers a nice photo opportunity.

Badger Bob tests his reading skills.

Turn left to Artist Point for an amazing view of the Grand Canyon of the Yellowstone.

Up and away. It's not as far as you think. After all was said and done, the French folks made it, and so will you. Freedom fries forever!

You made it. Congratulations! Good job! The views are indescribable. What more can be said?

It's worth a trip to the edge to see why it's called the Grand Canyon of the Yellowstone.

Badger Bob eschewed the trip to the edge by claiming he was giddy with the beauty of the spot [and not petrified of falling, screaming, into the canyon].

The Yellowstone River runs north. Very unusual for a river!

Have you seen enough? Take your time. You may make this hike only once in your life.

Now it's time to head back to the trailhead and break out the cooler. Snacks and beverages will be welcome. On the way, there is time to muse on this hike. How many different senses did you use? What impressed you most? Was the scenery awesome? Was this hike worth the effort? This trek is a smorgasbord of scenery, experiences, and beauty. What more could you ask for?

Memories are made of this.

Smiles and luck to you.

Lava Creek, Wraith Falls and Undine Falls

This is a two stage hike that is accessed from two different trailheads.

To reach Wraith Falls trailhead, take the highway from Mammoth to Tower Falls. Drive five [5] miles east. Pull in the Wraith Falls parking area on the right [south] side of the road. One half [½] mile before you reach the Wraith Falls trailhead, you will pass by Lava Creek picnic area. Remember this spot because this is where the Undine Falls trailhead is located. You will be coming back here for the second section of this hike.

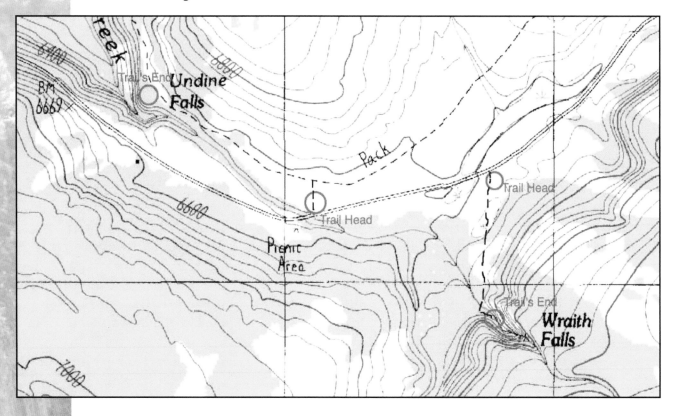

This hike is done in two stages with a double bonus. The first bonus is a great view of two waterfalls from two different viewpoints. The second bonus is seeing the high country without all the **up** hiking. It is a win, win situation.

The first stage of the hike is an easy one half [½] mile walk to see a beautiful waterfall that's not really a waterfall. It's more like an eighty-foot cascade. The second stage of the hike takes you to a true waterfall. You will get to see this waterfall from two different viewpoints. Plus, you will also see the cascade you just visited, from a different perspective.

The Professor mused, "Two viewpoints for two impressive features, I like it!"

Wraith Falls flows over an eighty foot rock face. It's quite a spectacle and it's easy to reach.

Look at the trees by the trail. The bison have left rub spots. The big animals use these trees as handy dandy scratching posts.

The missing tree bark lets you know the bison have been to see Wraith Falls before you.

A mixture of wild flowers catches your eye during the summer.

The Professor was impressed with a different type of cinquefoil. It's called shrubby cinquefoil (Potentilla friiticosa). This shrub-like plant has small yellow flowers. These flowers resemble the flowers of its cinquefoil relatives.

On the trail you may meet some interesting and friendly hikers who are ready to share their Yellowstone experiences with you. Park visitors like to share stories of animal sightings, thermal activity, or beautiful scenery.

It is not unusual to meet and make new friends in Yellowstone that can last a lifetime. It usually starts with a "Hello, where are you from and what have you seen?"

Shrubby Cinquefoil

Here the Badger and Mrs. Bob greet some folks from Minnesota.

A boardwalk bridge gets you across the muck! It will keep your feet high and dry while you cross. Check out the plant life on either side of the boardwalk bridge. Notice how the plants are different from the plants you have seen along the trail.

Some folks claim they don't see many animals on the trail. Maybe they don't look closely or maybe they are just looking for the big guys. Badger Bob and the Mrs. saw a short-tailed weasel (ermine) and a red squirrel on this hike.

Weasel

Red Squirrel

The Professor and his camera receive a chattery trail welcome from a local resident.

Badger Bob noticed the bright colored wildflowers. It seems the color of the day is yellow.

The wooden bridge signals your goal is near.

It's quite a sight, looking up at Wraith Falls from the viewing platform beneath it. Keep this picture in mind, because in the next stage of the hike you will see Wraith Falls from a different perspective.

Did you notice the water is rolling down the rock face of the incline?

In a true waterfall, the water would be free falling from the incline.

Do you think this feature is a waterfall or a cascade?

You are almost back to your rig.

Undine Falls from the viewing stand.

Head west three quarters [¾] of a mile to the Undine Falls overlook. Don't stop at the Lava creek picnic area yet. Park your rig and walk down to the overlook. Take a peek at Undine Falls. Enjoy the view.

Badger Bob peers over the friendly crowd to see Undine Falls.

A photograph of Undine Falls, as seen through a telephoto lens from the viewing platform. Impressive huh?

Lava Creek Trail to Undine Falls – the last stage of this hike.

Get back in your rig and drive east about a quarter [¼] of a mile to the Lava Creek picnic area parking lot. Pull in and park. Get your gear and check it out again. Slip on your pack, and you are ready to go. LOCK YOUR CAR AND SECURE YOUR KEYS. TELL A PAL WHERE YOU KEEP A SPARE KEY.

It's time to get down the trail and up to the plateau. The trailhead is located across the road [north] and then across the bridge [east].

Cross the bridge, take a quick left [north], and head up the

path onto the plateau. You are now on the backcountry trail.

Hike up the small incline.

Notice how things can change in only one year! Maybe next year a new sign will be here.

Sign in 2008

Sign in 2009

It's difficult to get lost if you watch for the Orange Trail markers. Do these trail signs give you a little clue?

"Go left, young Geezer, go left!"

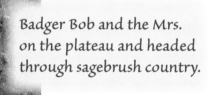

Badger Bob and the Mrs. on the plateau and headed through sagebrush country.

Gorgeous mountains dominate the western landscape. Sepulcher is the big boy in the foreground with Electric Peak behind it. Both of these behemoths are climbable!

Badger Bob shook his old grey head and muttered, "Not by me!"

Ten minutes on the trail and it's time to pull a Crazy Ivan (180° turn and view). Do you see an old friend in the distance? It's Wraith Falls. It looks quite different from this angle.

On the north side of the trail there's a dead man standing. Take a closer look at this tree. What happened to it? Was it fire, bugs, old age? What do you think?

Can you smell the sagebrush? Rub some with your hands then you will definitely smell it. Did you know that sagebrush is related to the Daisy?

The scientific name for this plant is Artimesia tridentata

This is the old viewing platform now closed by the Park Service. Now the only way to see the falls up close is from this back country trail!

Across the canyon, the new viewing platform is filled with curious visitors. These folks are looking at Undine Falls from the overlook where you were earlier.

Take another look at the brink of Undine Falls from the north side of the canyon.

"Hey! Not too close. Be careful."

On this side you can get closer to the falls!

Here's a photo opportunity you won't get from the viewing platform.

The backcountry view of Undine Falls is impressive. Ask the guy beside you what he thinks. Hey, there's no one beside you — that's because you're in the backcountry!

How do you like the out-back so far?

Looking south across the canyon, do you see what appears to be columnar basalt walls on the canyon face? What caused this?

What is columnar basalt anyway?

The Professor was silent, but not Badger Bob, "Where is a good geologist when you need one"?

Mountains galore!

Look at Electric Peak and Sepulcher, with Mammoth terrace in the foreground. It's a great treat to see these panoramic views after just a short walk in the backcountry.

Do you feel like you are on top of the world?

Turn your gaze west and take a good look at Lava Creek Canyon.

What a view!

Badger Bob asked the Professor to take a photo of "elk scat" to show there are elk on the north side of the canyon.

*The Professor was not happy, but it **was** evidence of elk presence. Badger Bob thought the elk might be watching people. "It could happen," said Badger Bob.*

Great views. Great hike. Great country. It doesn't get much better than this.

Badger Bob heads back to the trailhead with dreams of a bull elk dancing in his head.

Hike Ten —

Cave Falls to Bechler Falls

The Cave Falls trail is in the southern part of Yellowstone Park in an area called the Bechler (pronounced "Bek-ler"). This section of the park is lower and more moist than other parts of Yellowstone.

It is less accessible and therefore less used by visitors. The Bechler has more waterfalls than the rest of the park, as well as stunning visuals and marvelous hikes. Hiking in Yellowstone wouldn't be complete without a trip to Bechler and a view of some of its waterfalls.

The trailhead to Cave Falls is reached from Ashton, Idaho via the intersection of highway 20 and highway 47. Head east from the intersection on highway 47. Drive through Ashton and on to Cave Falls [about 24 miles].

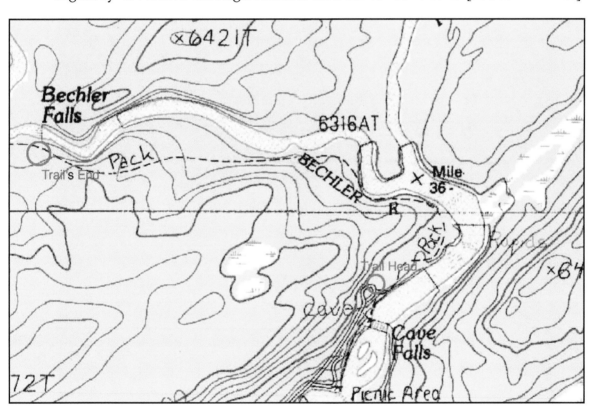

Stay on 47 and look for a sharp right bend in the road heading north. Take the first right [east]. This is Cave Falls road. This road takes you all the way to the Cave Falls trailhead. The road is gravel for about 10 miles and paved for the last 3 miles to Cave Falls. Follow the short loop to the parking area.

Park your rig, and check your gear. LOCK THE CAR AND SECURE YOUR KEYS. MAKE SURE A PAL HAS A SPARE KEY.

Take your camera and get some photos of Cave Falls before you start your hike.

Cave Falls on the Falls River.

The Trail Head is clearly marked.

Badger Bob surveyed the Falls River and adjusted his psyche for the hike ahead. The Professor hoped the proper motivation and commitment would be forth coming.

[Good luck, Professor].

The trail follows the river with woodlands on the other side. The river is topped with glistening white water on its way to the ocean.

If you are talking with a companion while you walk, you'll find yourself shouting. If you are singing as you hike, you may need a megaphone to make yourself heard.

The Fall River's music is lovely but it is also very loud.

The power of the flowing water in the Falls River is awesome.

The Professor captured an eddy with his camera.

Islands in the Stream.

A short distance up the trail you'll spot an island in
the Falls River. Note the logjam where the current meets the island.

Fireweed *[epilobium angustifo-lium]* on the Falls River adds
color and texture to the view.

Badger Bob considers the confluence of the Bechler and Falls Rivers.

White water abounds at the meeting of the two rivers.

This is a spectacular sight, yet few visitors take the time to come and see this beauty.

Now it's time to adjust your trail legs for a little up. Your lungs will dictate the pace.

You are hiking in the forest but the river doesn't lose its voice. It just sings a little softer.

Onward and upward to Bechler Falls.

Trees may hide the view, but not the sound of the river.

The Bechler seems calm at this point, but who knows what's ahead?

Badger Bob examines a bump on a tree. The Professor explained that the knot is called a burl.

More islands in the stream complete with log jams.

Is this a combination of many old logjams or recent evidence of spring run off at work?

There it is! The first view of Bechler Falls through the trees.

It took less than 45 minutes of light hiking to get here.

Aquatic greetings. You have now arrived at Bechler Falls.

Time for a break! Drop your pack and lean your trekking poles against a tree. Break out the beverages and goodies.

You did it! Well done. After the food and beverage break it's time for a nap or a photo shoot. You may not get here again so take your time and enjoy yourself.

Naptime is over and the snacks are low, so it may be time to head back. Please be sure to pick up any trash or debris left in the area, even if it isn't yours. Some thoughtless or immature trail hand may have left it or dropped it. The next trekker will have a better back-country experience, and it will be because of your efforts.

"Thank you!" says Badger Bob for all the hikers yet to come this way.

This is an amazing place!

Take it all in Badger Bob! Let the river soak into you for a change.

The Trailhead is in sight and this hike is in the bag. Congratulations! You have done it. This experience may awaken the trekker inside you and inspire you to take more walks on the wild side. The real treasures are the sights and sounds of the backcountry. You now have the experience filed away in your head. The number of folks who will enjoy hearing about your trail experiences may pleasantly surprise you.

Long life to you!